CELTA MADE EASY

The Ultimate Guide to Surviving and
Succeeding on Your CELTA Course

Daniel James

CONTENTS

Title Page
Introduction
Pre-CELTA Study Plan – Your 30-Day Warm-Up   1
Chapter 1: What to Expect on CELTA   5
Chapter 2: Surviving the First Weeks   11
Chapter 3: The CELTA Assignments – How I Passed   17
Chapter 4: Lesson Planning Like a Pro   23
Chapter 5: Dealing With Feedback and Reflection   29
Chapter 6: Tools and Templates That Saved Me   34
Chapter 7: Time Management and Burnout Prevention   39
Chapter 8: Life After CELTA   44
Chapter 9: Bonus Tools and Templates   49
Bonus Chapter: Trainer Secrets – What CELTA Tutors Really Look For   53
Enjoyed This Book? Please Leave a 5-Star Review   56
Books By This Author   57

INTRODUCTION

The CELTA course is often described as one of the most intense and transformative teacher training experiences available to aspiring English language teachers. For many, it is a rite of passage—a four-week crucible of lesson planning, peer teaching, self-reflection, and constant evaluation. But while the Cambridge CELTA is standardized and globally respected, what it feels like to go through it varies immensely from person to person. That's why this book exists.

CELTA Made Easy: The Ultimate Guide is not written by a training provider or academic. It is written by a real CELTA graduate who not only survived the course, but also meticulously documented the highs, lows, strategies, and slip-ups that made the difference. Every lesson plan, assignment, piece of feedback, and moment of doubt has been mined and reshaped here into something useful—for you.

Since completing the CELTA, I have gone on to work as an IELTS examiner, author multiple IELTS preparation books including *IELTS Speaking 101* and *Band 7+ Idioms & Phrasal Verbs*, and secure a position as an Assistant Professor at a major university in South Korea. CELTA wasn't just a course; it was the springboard that launched a career.

This book is designed to be a *pre-course companion* and an *in-course survival manual*. It doesn't rehash Cambridge content. Instead, it gives you a grounded, honest, and practical understanding of what you're walking into. More importantly, it shows you how to walk out stronger and more confident.

Who This Book Is For

- CELTA candidates preparing to start the course.
- Trainees currently on the course who feel overwhelmed.
- Teachers considering CELTA and wondering what it really involves.
- Anyone who wants real insights into how to plan lessons, reflect critically, and manage the mental load of intensive teacher training.

What Makes This Book Different

Unlike official CELTA handbooks or online forums full of general advice, this guide is built from direct, lived experience. Every teaching practice (TP), assignment, reflection, and course component discussed is drawn from authentic experience. You'll find:

- Real lesson plans annotated with post-lesson reflections
- Honest accounts of what went wrong (and right)
- Clear examples of how I passed the four assignments
- Tools and techniques I used to stay organized and sane
- Guidance on how to think like a successful trainee

Why Write This Book?

When I began my CELTA, I quickly realized that most resources out there were either too vague, too theoretical, or too generic to offer meaningful help. There were plenty of YouTube videos and Reddit threads, but few took you inside the course from the learner's perspective—with actual reflections, actual TP struggles, and actual tutor feedback.

I decided to change that.

My goal with this book is simple: to demystify the CELTA and help you not just pass, but excel. With clear examples and actionable strategies, this book will help you:

- Navigate the workload more efficiently
- Prepare for assignments with purpose
- Teach lessons that actually meet the assessment criteria
- Understand the mindset trainers are looking for

If you're looking for a polished, professional edge without the jargon or fluff, you're in the right place.

Let's begin.

PRE-CELTA STUDY PLAN – YOUR 30-DAY WARM-UP

Many candidates arrive at CELTA with strong motivation but limited preparation. If you want to walk into Day 1 with clarity, confidence, and an edge, this 30-day pre-course plan will help you get there. It's not about mastering everything in advance—it's about developing familiarity so you can absorb new input faster and reduce decision fatigue in your first weeks.

This plan focuses on four key pillars:

1. Grammar knowledge
2. Phonology basics
3. Teaching terminology
4. Lesson structure awareness

Week 1: Build Your Grammar Foundation

Focus: Tense review, basic terminology, identifying form

Tasks:

- Watch 2–3 grammar explainer videos (Perfect English

Grammar or BBC Learning English)
- Create a one-page tense timeline chart (present, past, future; simple, continuous, perfect)
- Study parts of speech and clause types (subject, object, etc.)
- Begin reading *Practical English Usage* by Michael Swan – 10 minutes a day

Outputs:

- Make flashcards for verb tenses and example sentences
- Write 3 MPF breakdowns for common forms (e.g. past simple, present perfect, 2nd conditional)

Week 2: Phonology and Pronunciation Awareness

Focus: Understanding stress, sounds, and connected speech

Tasks:

- Study the phonemic chart (British Council website or Adrian Underhill videos)
- Learn how to transcribe basic words (e.g. /ˈkæt/, /həˈləʊ/)
- Practice identifying word stress in polysyllabic words
- Learn weak forms, schwa /ə/, and intonation basics

Outputs:

- Transcribe 10 words you use daily
- Practice reading 5 sentences with contrastive stress and connected speech
- Watch 3 pronunciation videos and take notes on stress/intonation

Week 3: Teaching Terminology & Lesson Logic

Focus: Understanding CELTA's language, lesson flow, and basic techniques

Tasks:

- Learn the acronyms: CCQ, ICQ, MPF, TTT, STT, L1, L2, PPP, TBL, etc.
- Watch a recorded ESL lesson (on YouTube or British Council Teaching English)
- Read 2 sample lesson plans from online CELTA prep books or forums
- Study classroom management language (e.g. "Turn to your partner," "Check together," "Compare your ideas")

Outputs:

- Define 10 key CELTA terms in your own words
- Annotate a sample lesson plan with your thoughts or questions

Week 4: Simulate the Experience

Focus: Applying your knowledge and building classroom instincts

Tasks:

- Choose 1 grammar point and write a short MPF analysis
- Watch 2–3 real CELTA TPs online (search "CELTA TP sample lesson" on YouTube)
- Try planning a mini lesson (10 minutes) with a lead-in, clarification, controlled task, and freer task
- Record yourself giving instructions or presenting a grammar point

Outputs:

- Write a 150-word reflection: "What did I learn about myself as a teacher this week?"

- Identify your top 3 areas of nervousness and note 1 strategy for each

Checkpoint: If you complete 60–70% of this plan, you will already be ahead of most CELTA trainees on Day 1. You'll recognise key terms, have internal frameworks to build on, and feel less overwhelmed when the course intensifies.

CHAPTER 1: WHAT TO EXPECT ON CELTA

Before you set foot inside your first CELTA session, you'll likely have been told it's intense. That it's hard work. That it will stretch you. All true—but vague. What they don't always explain is why it feels that way, or how the course actually runs from day to day.

Let me walk you through what you can expect—honestly, practically, and with the benefit of hindsight.

The CELTA Course in a Nutshell

CELTA is a Cambridge-accredited teaching qualification designed to prepare people to teach English to speakers of other languages. Whether you're coming into it with years of teaching experience or none at all, CELTA is designed to challenge, reshape, and professionalize how you think about teaching.

It comprises three core elements:

- **Teaching Practice (TP):** You teach real students, usually in 40-minute lessons, under observation.
- **Input Sessions:** You receive training on language systems, skills, methodology, and classroom techniques.

- **Written Assignments:** Four assessed pieces that show your understanding of learners, language, skills, and your development.

That may sound manageable, but what makes CELTA intense isn't the number of components—it's the **speed, the scrutiny, and the steep learning curve.**

The Daily Reality

The daily rhythm of CELTA looks something like this:
- **Morning:** Input sessions with trainers (theory, methods, grammar, phonology)
- **Afternoon:** Teaching Practice (or observation), followed by feedback
- **Evening:** Lesson planning, assignment writing, and trying to stay afloat

If you're on a full-time course, this schedule repeats five days a week for four weeks. On part-time or online formats (like mine), the intensity is spread out—but the workload remains.

From My Schedule (Oxford TEFL – Online)

Every Saturday, we had TP and feedback sessions from 10:00–15:30. During the week, we completed self-study modules, attended live Zoom input sessions, and submitted lesson plans or assignments. It felt like juggling spinning plates—one wobble, and everything could fall.

This is what I wish someone had told me early on:

> "It's not about surviving the CELTA. It's about **learning how to learn under pressure**, how to teach with purpose, and how to reflect like a professional."

Teaching Practice: Where

You're Made or Broken

Teaching Practice (TP) is the heart of CELTA—and the most nerve-wracking component. You'll teach to a real group of adult learners, often alongside two or three other trainees, rotating lessons each day.

You'll be assessed on:

- How clearly you present language or skills
- Whether your students meet the lesson aims
- Classroom presence and instruction
- Awareness of timing, interaction, and engagement

My first TP was rough. I overplanned, overspoke, and under-elicited. I clung to my PowerPoint and barely monitored the room. But the experience of actually *doing it*, of seeing students respond (or not respond) to what I had prepared—that was the turning point.

By TP5, I had learned how to:

- Use CCQs and ICQs fluently
- Write more focused aims
- Time activities better
- Give space for students to speak and self-correct

> **Trainee Tip:** Record yourself teaching—even if it's awkward. You'll pick up on nervous habits, pacing issues, and tone of voice that aren't always obvious in the moment.

The Written Assignments

There are four written assignments, each 750–1,000 words:

1. **Focus on the Learner** – Analyse a student's strengths/needs
2. **Language Related Tasks** – Deconstruct grammar,

vocabulary, pronunciation
3. **Skills-Related Task** – Create a lesson around a reading or listening text
4. **Lessons from the Classroom** – Reflect on your development across the course

These aren't difficult in theory, but each requires *precision, clarity, and self-awareness*. Rewrites are common. I had to rewrite one. It's not failure—it's part of the process.

> **Trainer Insight:** "We're not looking for essays. We're looking for informed, practical analysis that shows you understand your learners and your teaching decisions."

Input Sessions: Theory Meets Practice

Input sessions are where you learn about language systems (grammar, lexis, phonology), lesson planning frameworks (PPP, TBL, Guided Discovery), and essential teaching practices like:

- Classroom management
- Eliciting
- Concept checking
- Staging activities

These sessions can feel like drinking from a fire hose—especially if you haven't studied grammar in years. Take notes. Review them. Ask questions.

The best sessions for me included:

- **Error correction strategies** – how to correct without undermining
- **Receptive skills lessons** – designing gist vs detail tasks
- **Using authentic materials** – how to adapt real texts

Why It Feels So Intense

CELTA doesn't just test your knowledge. It tests your **resilience**, your **time management**, your **ability to respond to feedback**, and your **willingness to change**. For four weeks (or more), you are:

- Planning under pressure
- Teaching under observation
- Reflecting under scrutiny

It's humbling—and that's the point. It strips away bad habits, lazy instincts, and ego. It pushes you toward professional clarity.

> **Trainee Reflection:** "I didn't know how little I knew until I stood in front of that class with my plan in one hand and my confidence in the other."

But So Is the Progress

What makes CELTA remarkable isn't just the stress—it's the *acceleration*. I watched my teaching skills evolve in real time. I started the course thinking I knew how to teach. I ended it *actually* knowing how to teach.

By the end, I was able to:

- Plan a lesson in under 90 minutes
- Predict and resolve learner problems
- Use language clarification techniques with confidence
- Reflect critically and constructively on my own performance

CELTA gave me the foundation I needed to:

- Work as an IELTS examiner
- Write books on IELTS Speaking and Vocabulary
- Teach at university level in South Korea

And it all began with teaching students how to talk about free time, superlatives, moral dilemmas, and idioms in my TP sessions.

What You'll Take With You

You won't remember every input session. But you'll never forget:

- The moment your students understood a difficult point
- The buzz after a successful freer practice
- The sting of a harsh (but fair) feedback session
- The sense of growth when your planning finally clicks

In the next chapter, I'll show you how to prepare before the course even begins—what to read, what to practice, and how to walk into CELTA with clarity and confidence.

CHAPTER 2: SURVIVING THE FIRST WEEKS

If you've ever felt overwhelmed in the first few days of a new job, imagine compressing that experience into a pedagogical boot camp where you're constantly assessed, critiqued, and expected to perform at your best in front of real students. That's CELTA.

For many candidates, the first two weeks are the most mentally taxing. You're adjusting to the structure, learning new terminology, managing live lessons, and realizing just how much you *don't* know about your own language. Add to that the anxiety of teaching your first real class, and you have a potent mix of pressure and uncertainty.

But here's the truth: *everyone feels this way*. The ones who thrive are the ones who learn how to manage that pressure, organize their workflow, and lean into the process rather than resist it.

The Shock Factor

I came into CELTA with prior teaching experience. I had taught university students in Korea and led IELTS prep classes. I thought

I'd be comfortable.

I wasn't.

CELTA makes you justify every minute of your lesson plan. Every activity, every instruction, every target structure has to serve a purpose—and be defensible in a post-lesson feedback session. That level of scrutiny was new.

In my first two weeks, I:

- Misjudged lesson timing
- Overused teacher talking time (TTT)
- Confused task setup with actual instruction
- Wrote vague aims and hoped they'd pass

None of this made me a bad teacher. It made me a typical trainee.

> **Trainer Insight:** "We don't expect perfection. We expect evidence that you're thinking, analysing, and learning. A good CELTA trainee isn't mistake-free. They're responsive."

Establishing a Routine

Routine became my shield. Without it, CELTA would have eaten me alive. Here's the pattern I established:

My Weekly Rhythm (Online CELTA)

- **07:30–08:30** – Review lesson objectives or feedback from previous session
- **09:00–12:00** – Live input sessions or self-study modules
- **12:00–13:00** – Lunch, reset, decompress
- **13:00–15:00** – Lesson plan prep or assignment work
- **15:00–17:00** – Zoom calls with peers or feedback review
- **Evening** – Finish any prep, practice ICQs/CCQs aloud, grammar drills

That routine gave me structure and stability. It also helped me identify what to prioritise and when to stop tweaking.

> **Trainee Tip:** Use time-blocking. Don't "work on the lesson plan tonight"—block out 18:30–20:00 to write your lead-in and controlled practice only. Small wins matter.

Emotional Management

No one warns you how emotionally intense CELTA is. On paper, it's about lesson planning and grammar. In reality, it's about handling vulnerability in front of strangers.

Here's what caught me off guard:

- Feeling exposed when my lesson didn't land
- Comparing myself to more confident trainees
- Taking feedback too personally

And here's what helped:

- Reframing feedback as coaching, not criticism
- Celebrating small victories ("my ICQs worked!")
- Talking openly with peers, who felt the same way

> **Trainer Insight:** "If you're *not* feeling vulnerable at some point during CELTA, you're probably not being honest with yourself. Growth feels uncomfortable. That's normal."

The First Teaching Practice (TP)

Your first TP isn't designed to be perfect—it's designed to get you teaching. My first assessed lesson (TP2) was a listening class on family vocabulary. I planned it meticulously… but forgot:

- To test my audio in Zoom breakout rooms
- To time the lead-in correctly
- To allow peer-checking before open class feedback

And yet... the students participated. They smiled. They answered questions. That's all I needed to keep going.

By TP5, I was confident enough to:

- Elicit naturally
- Use concept-checking questions fluidly
- Time my activities within a minute or two
- Let students take centre stage during freer practice

Trainee Reflection: "The gap between knowing what to do and being able to do it under pressure is where the real CELTA happens."

How I Handled Feedback

In Chapter 5 we'll go into detail, but here's the key point:

I stopped fearing feedback the moment I started predicting it.

If you know you spoke too much or skipped instructions, *say it first* during reflection. This builds trust with your tutor and shows real self-awareness.

- Don't say "I think it went okay."
- Say "I think the lead-in was too long and affected my controlled practice timing."

The difference is huge.

Imposter Syndrome Is Common

Everyone on your CELTA course will have moments of self-doubt —yes, even the confident ones. Especially in the first two weeks.

If you're asking yourself:

- "Am I good enough for this?"
- "Why can't I get this aim right?"

- "Do I even understand what scaffolding is?"

You're not alone. You're *normal*. And you're exactly the kind of person who succeeds—if you keep showing up.

Halfway Through: The Turning Point

Something shifts when you reach the middle of the course. Your understanding deepens. You:

- Recognize strong vs weak aims
- Use CCQs without overexplaining
- Reflect with accuracy
- Plan faster

You start teaching with more awareness and less guesswork. It's not easy, but it's working.

Checkpoint: By the mid point, you should be:

- Planning lessons under 3 hours
- Using MPF for new language
- Giving clear instructions 80% of the time
- Receiving less correction and more development-focused feedback

If you're not there yet? That's okay too. Some of my cohort didn't find their rhythm until TP6 or later—and they still passed with flying colours.

Self-Care Is Non-Negotiable

You cannot perform under pressure if you don't rest. Here's what I built into my week:

- **One night off completely**: no CELTA talk, no lesson plans
- **Daily walks**: reset the nervous system
- **Food planning**: CELTA is not the time to start intermittent fasting

You don't win CELTA by burning out. You win it by *lasting the course.*

> **Trainee Tip:** Create a "non-CELTA" chat with friends or family. You'll need space to remember who you are outside the course.

In the next chapter, we'll explore how I tackled the four CELTA assignments—what I got right, where I stumbled, and how you can save time while still hitting the criteria.

CHAPTER 3: THE CELTA ASSIGNMENTS – HOW I PASSED

While Teaching Practice gets the spotlight on CELTA, the four written assignments are the hidden pressure points of the course. Each one is short—just 750 to 1,000 words—but deceptively rigorous. They test your ability to reflect, analyse, and apply what you're learning in real time.

In this chapter, I'll walk you through each assignment: what it is, what I submitted, what went wrong (and right), and the strategies I used to pass.

Assignment 1: Focus on the Learner

What It Involves

You choose one of your learners from Teaching Practice and gather data about their background, strengths, weaknesses, and learning preferences. You then analyse a short writing or speaking sample and suggest targeted strategies to help them improve.

This assignment tests how well you can identify real learner needs, link them to specific language issues, and make pedagogically sound recommendations.

My Experience

I selected a student from Saudi Arabia who was confident in speaking but made consistent grammar errors when writing, especially with articles and verb tenses. I conducted a brief interview and asked him to write about his daily routine.

My first draft was far too descriptive. I spent too much time talking about what the student *liked* instead of focusing on what they *needed*. It wasn't until my second draft that I really honed in on the language analysis.

What Worked

- I used direct examples from his writing, like "He go to office at 8" and "He like watch TV."
- I recommended practical activities like substitution drills, noticing tasks, and using a learner diary.
- I highlighted the student's motivation level and how that could be leveraged.

What Didn't

- I originally ignored phonological issues entirely.
- My learning strategies were too vague—"practice more" isn't good enough on CELTA.

Trainee Tip: Use actual learner sentences. The stronger your examples, the easier it is to make clear recommendations.

Assignment 2: Language Related Tasks

What It Involves

This is the most technical assignment. You're given four pieces of target language—typically tenses, modals, or phrases—and asked

to analyse:
- Meaning
- Form
- Pronunciation (including phonemic script and sentence stress)
- Potential learner problems

It's a test of your own language awareness, and many trainees (myself included) underestimate it.

My Experience

I tackled phrases like "I've been working here for two years" and "used to live." I initially wrote surface-level answers like "This is the present perfect continuous." My tutor was clear: naming the tense is not enough. You must explain **what it conveys, how it functions, and how you'll teach it.**

What Worked

- I created timelines for each tense.
- I wrote CCQs for each form (e.g., "Did the action start in the past?" "Is it still happening now?").
- I analysed the phonology, including weak forms and connected speech.

What Didn't

- My first pronunciation section lacked stress patterns and intonation.
- I didn't initially address *why* students might misuse certain forms (e.g., L1 interference).

    Trainer Insight: "You're not just showing us you know the grammar—you're showing us you know how to teach it to someone who doesn't."

Assignment 3: Skills-Related Task

What It Involves

You analyse a reading or listening text (authentic or adapted) and design a lesson around it. You need to:

- Justify your choice of text
- Outline the sub-skills you're targeting (e.g., skimming, scanning)
- Describe pre-, while-, and post-activities
- Anticipate learner difficulties

This is where many trainees fall into the trap of designing a comprehension test rather than a skills lesson.

My Experience

I chose a reading text on moral dilemmas from a graded reader. I designed a gist task, a detailed reading task, and a discussion activity at the end.

What worked:

- I clearly identified the sub-skills and justified their inclusion.
- I anticipated learner difficulty with idiomatic language in the text.
- My lesson stages were clear and logically sequenced.

What didn't:

- I initially ignored the opportunity for a *language focus* at the end.
- My post-task was too open—students needed more guidance.

   Trainee Tip: Always ask yourself, "Am I helping students develop skills, or am I just testing comprehension?"

Assignment 4: Lessons from the Classroom

What It Involves

This reflective piece asks you to chart your development across the course. You need to select two or three areas of your teaching that have improved, using examples from your TPs to support your analysis.

It's less technical—but it's still assessed, and superficial answers won't pass.

My Experience

I focused on three areas:

- Reducing TTT
- Improving instruction clarity
- Developing classroom presence

Because I had written post-lesson reflections after every TP, I had plenty of material to draw on.

What Worked

- I quoted from my own reflections to show development over time.
- I used specific lessons (e.g., TP2 and TP7) to show contrast.
- I explained *how* feedback shaped my decisions in future lessons.

What Didn't

- My first draft lacked reference to the CELTA assessment criteria.
- I made general statements like "I felt more confident" without backing them up.

   Trainee Tip: Think like a portfolio builder. What evidence do you have of growth? What changed? Why?

Common Mistakes and How to Avoid Them

Don't:

- Treat the assignments like academic essays
- Write overly long background sections
- Skip the learner perspective
- Avoid tutor feedback on drafts

Do:

- Link everything to teaching practice
- Anticipate problems as a teacher, not a student
- Include language examples, timelines, and phonemic scripts
- Ask for support before submitting a second draft

    Checkpoint: If you're spending more than 6–8 hours per assignment, you may be overthinking it. Clarity beats complexity every time.

In the next chapter, I'll take you inside how I planned my TPs—from adapting coursebook tasks to managing timing and student interaction. You'll see how my planning style evolved and how I avoided the common traps that trip up even confident trainees.

CHAPTER 4: LESSON PLANNING LIKE A PRO

Lesson planning on CELTA is a different beast from planning in the real world. During the course, every lesson is scrutinized—not just for what you teach, but how and why you teach it. A CELTA plan isn't just a teaching script—it's a demonstration of your awareness, clarity, and strategic thinking.

Here's how I approached lesson planning—and how you can too.

What CELTA Tutors Expect

At minimum, your plan must clearly show:

- A logical aim (communicative or language-based)
- Stage-by-stage breakdown of tasks and timings
- Interaction patterns (T-S, S-S, S-S-S, etc.)
- Anticipated problems and solutions
- Language analysis using MPF (Meaning, Pronunciation, Form)
- ICQs and CCQs to check instructions and understanding

These documents often run 3–6 pages long, depending on the complexity of your aims. Some trainees find this frustrating—but CELTA isn't assessing you as a finished teacher. It's assessing your thinking. If your plan is coherent, teachable, and anticipates learner needs, you're in a strong position.

Trainee Tip: Start every plan with this question: "What should students be able to do at the end of this lesson that they couldn't do before?"

How I Planned Each TP

Like most trainees, I overplanned in the beginning. My early lessons were packed with stages, activities, backup materials, and long explanations. It wasn't until TP4 that I started to understand how to simplify without weakening the aim.

Here's a breakdown of key lessons that shaped my growth.

TP4: Vocabulary (Free Time)

Level: A2
Main Aim: Vocabulary – free time activities
Sub Aim: Collocations

This lesson taught lexis like watch TV, do sport, go shopping, visit friends. I used visuals, matching tasks, and a collocation sort (e.g., go swimming vs do yoga). The timing was tight, but it was the first lesson where I started to feel in control.

What worked:

- Clear MPF stages
- Engaging visuals
- Functional controlled practice

What didn't:

- Too many slides
- Weak instruction checking

TP5: Grammar (Superlatives)

Level: B1

Main Aim: Grammar – superlatives
Sub Aim: Speaking fluency

This class used real-world contexts (brands, restaurants, travel) to teach forms like the best, the most interesting, the worst. I tied the grammar to a discussion-based freer practice.

What worked:

- Strong context and lead-in
- Natural speaking prompts
- Time allocation felt tight but achievable

What didn't:

- I underestimated how long students would need for pair-work debriefs
- My boardwork (on Zoom) was messy and rushed

TP6: Reading (Moral Dilemmas)

Level: B1
Main Aim: Reading for gist and detail
Sub Aim: Vocabulary (discourse markers)

I used an adapted authentic text about a student who faces a dilemma. Students predicted, read for gist, answered comprehension questions, and then discussed what they would do.

What worked:

- Clear skills staging (pre-task, while-task, post-task)
- I made space for student ideas
- Meaningful discussion emerged

What didn't:

- Pre-teaching was slightly too long
- I didn't account for the emotional weight of the topic—some learners were quiet

Trainer Insight: A good receptive skills lesson is less about giving the answers and more about helping learners develop strategies to get there themselves.

TP7: Listening (TED Talk – Secrets of Success)

Level: B2
Main Aim: Listening for gist and detail
Sub Aim: Speaking fluency

This lesson almost fell apart. I chose a fast-paced TED Talk and added subtitles last-minute—this undermined my listening aim. I also had screen-sharing issues and lost 7 minutes troubleshooting.

What worked:

- Good idea, poor execution
- Engaging content with relevant vocabulary

What didn't:

- Tech failed
- My pacing was off
- I felt rattled during feedback

Lessons learned:

- Always rehearse tech-heavy lessons
- Don't make last-minute changes
- Plan fallback tasks in case something fails

TP8: Vocabulary (Idioms)

Level: B2
Main Aim: Vocabulary – idiomatic expressions
Sub Aim: Contextual speaking

This lesson focused on expressions like cost an arm and a leg, hold your horses, and gut feeling. I used matching activities, context fill-ins, and a storytelling freer practice.

What worked:

- Engaging and memorable examples
- Personal storytelling helped clarify idioms
- Students reused the idioms naturally

What didn't:

- I rushed the freer task setup
- I needed to monitor more actively during the final discussion

Trainee Tip: Keep your plan realistic. It's better to teach three idioms well than six poorly.

Planning Lessons That Work

After TP4, I started using my own reusable templates:

- Stage-by-stage lesson skeleton (Aim → Procedure → Timing → Interaction → Rationale)
- Language Analysis Grid (MPF + CCQs + Problems/Solutions)
- Lesson reflection tracker (Plan vs reality, student reactions, feedback quotes)

These systems cut my planning time by 30–40 percent and gave me confidence. Once you know the structure, you can focus on how you're teaching—not just ticking boxes.

Trainee Tip: The more you plan, the more natural it becomes. By TP7, I could build an entire lesson skeleton in under 20 minutes.

Common Planning Pitfalls

- Trying to be too original. Stick with tried-and-tested frameworks. Save experimentation for after CELTA.
- Underestimating time. If you think a stage will take five minutes, it will probably take eight. Always plan buffer time.

- Ignoring student roles. Your plan must include time for pair-checking, group work, and student-led feedback.
- Forgetting rationale. If you can't justify an activity in one sentence, it probably doesn't belong.

Checkpoint: Your lesson plan is complete if:

- Every stage supports your main aim
- Every task has clear instructions and ICQs
- You've identified two or more realistic learner difficulties
- You can confidently explain your decisions during feedback

In the next chapter, I'll show you what happens after the plan is delivered—how to survive feedback, reflect effectively, and turn even the worst lesson into fuel for improvement.

CHAPTER 5: DEALING WITH FEEDBACK AND REFLECTION

One of the most emotionally charged aspects of the CELTA course is the feedback session. After every Teaching Practice (TP), you sit with your tutor and fellow trainees to analyse what worked—and what didn't. It's not just a post-lesson chat. It is a structured, focused critique designed to develop you as a teacher under pressure.

Some lessons will go well. Others won't. But every session is an opportunity to improve—if you know how to process the experience productively.

Understanding the Feedback Structure

CELTA feedback follows a set routine:

- Each trainee begins by reflecting on their own performance.
- Peers offer their comments.
- The tutor delivers feedback, highlighting both strengths and areas for development.

These sessions often take place in small groups immediately after the teaching block. While the tone is professional, the impact can be personal—especially early in the course when confidence is fragile.

My Early Experience With Feedback

In my first two TPs, I found the process disorienting. I knew the lessons weren't perfect, but hearing the issues presented aloud in front of others felt exposing. I realised quickly that this discomfort was normal.

What mattered most was how I responded:

- I wrote down every piece of feedback.
- I summarised the feedback into themes.
- I began each new lesson plan by reviewing my last feedback sheet.

Over time, this transformed my performance. By TP5, my tutor was noting improvements that directly linked to previous sessions. The loop of performance → feedback → adjustment became my development engine.

Self-Reflection: From Obligation to Opportunity

After every TP, you are required to submit a self-reflection. This isn't busywork. It is a record of your ability to self-evaluate, spot patterns, and link outcomes to decisions made during planning and delivery.

A strong reflection:

- Describes what happened without excessive narrative.
- Identifies what worked well and why.
- Analyses what didn't work and offers alternatives.
- Links teaching practice to CELTA assessment criteria.

Sample reflection excerpt:

"Today's class was my best so far. I felt more confident with timing, and students responded well to my freer practice task. However, I still need to work on giving clearer task instructions. I noticed students hesitated during setup, which suggests my ICQs were ineffective."

Compare that to a weaker example:

"The lesson was OK. Some students looked confused. I think it was fine, but it could have been better."

The difference is clarity, ownership, and professionalism.

How to Make Feedback Work for You

1. Be honest in your self-reflection. If you know a stage went poorly, say so first. It shows awareness and maturity.
2. Identify repeated patterns in your feedback. If the same issue appears twice, make it a priority. In my case, excessive TTT and weak lead-ins were flagged consistently. Once I addressed them, my overall performance improved dramatically.
3. Don't debate the feedback. Ask clarifying questions, but avoid defensiveness. Tutors are not interested in excuses —they are watching for growth.
4. Document your development. I kept a separate file that logged my feedback trends, target areas, and examples of improvement. This helped immensely when writing Assignment 4 (Lessons from the Classroom).

Trainer Insight: Growth on CELTA is not linear. One week you'll feel in control, the next you'll feel like a beginner again. That is normal. What matters is how you reflect and adjust.

Peer Feedback: A Hidden Asset

Many trainees overlook peer feedback, either out of politeness or fear of giving offence. But learning to give and receive constructive comments is a professional skill.

Good peer feedback is:

- Specific: "Your lead-in was clear and engaging."
- Balanced: "You monitored well, but I think your boardwork could be clearer."
- Practical: "Consider using fewer examples to save time during clarification."

I learned as much from watching my peers teach as I did from teaching myself. Seeing their successes and struggles helped me understand the range of effective styles—and the importance of clarity regardless of personality.

Trainee Tip: Watching others helps you realise you're not alone. Everyone has a weak TP. Everyone forgets a CCQ. Use your cohort as a mirror, not a measurement.

Turning Mistakes Into Growth

One of my most difficult lessons was TP7. Technical issues disrupted my listening lesson. I lost control of the timing. I missed key opportunities to engage learners. The feedback was tough, but fair.

I could have walked away disheartened. Instead, I:

- Rewatched the lesson recording.
- Identified the moment I lost my flow.
- Created a checklist to avoid the same tech pitfalls.

By TP8, my final lesson was structured, confident, and well-paced. The same tutor who had been critical earlier noted the transformation. That progression would never have happened without reflection and action.

Key Reflection Questions

Use these to structure your self-assessment after each lesson:

1. Did I achieve my aim? Why or why not?
2. Which stage went best, and what made it work?
3. Where did students struggle, and how did I respond?
4. What feedback am I expecting today? How can I use it?

Checkpoint: If your post-lesson reflections by TP5 are still vague or purely emotional, it's time to refine your language. You are not just processing feelings—you are developing professional insight.

In the next chapter, we'll look at the tools, templates, and planning systems that helped me save time, stay sane, and deliver better lessons under pressure.

CHAPTER 6: TOOLS AND TEMPLATES THAT SAVED ME

One of the biggest challenges on CELTA is not just the content—it's the pace. You are constantly planning, writing, reflecting, adapting. Without systems in place, the workload can overwhelm even the most organised trainee.

This chapter shares the practical tools, habits, and templates I used to save time, reduce stress, and improve the quality of my teaching.

Lesson Planning Templates

By TP4, I realised I needed reusable frameworks. Every CELTA lesson follows a basic rhythm:

- Lead-in
- Clarification (for grammar or vocabulary)
- Controlled practice
- Freer practice
- Feedback and wrap-up

To avoid rebuilding the wheel each time, I created a digital template that included:

1. **Lesson Skeleton:**
- Stage name
- Aim of the stage
- Timing
- Interaction pattern (T-S, S-S, etc.)
- Procedure
- Notes or rationale

2. **Language Analysis Sheet:** For each target item:
- Meaning (with CCQs)
- Form (grammar structure breakdown)
- Pronunciation (phonemic script, stress, intonation)
- Common learner problems and solutions

Having these completed in advance helped me focus on tailoring each lesson, rather than reformatting or worrying about what I might forget.

Trainee Tip: Create your own personal template by Week 2. Don't rely solely on the CELTA-issued planning documents—they are comprehensive but not efficient.

Digital Tools I Used Every Day

These tools helped me stay organised, especially on the online course:

- **Google Docs:** Used for writing assignments, lesson plans, and reflections. Shared with tutors for easy feedback.
- **Google Drive:** I created folders by week, lesson type, and assignment. Organisation matters when you are juggling multiple inputs.
- **Google Sheets:** I built a simple tracker for deadlines, TPs, assignment stages, and input session highlights.
- **Canva:** For designing visuals, timelines, or simplified

boardwork (especially useful when teaching online).
- **YouTube:** I used grammar explanation videos to clarify target language and understand how others presented it.

Timing Tools

Lesson timing was a constant challenge in the early weeks. I consistently overran or under-ran tasks. To fix this, I used:

- A stopwatch during planning rehearsals.
- A visible timer during teaching to manage individual stages.
- Post-lesson notes on how long stages actually took versus my estimates.

This data helped me adjust pacing and be more realistic in my planning.

Trainer Insight: Under-planning is rare on CELTA. Over-planning is common. Timing problems often stem from trying to do too much, not too little.

My Personal Planning Workflow

By the midpoint of the course, I followed a simple planning routine:

1. **Review tutor feedback from last lesson.** What do I need to fix?
2. **Clarify my aim.** Write it in one sentence: "Students will practice the present perfect through a reading text and discussion."
3. **Choose or adapt material.** Find a coursebook page or authentic text that supports that aim.
4. **Complete language analysis.** Break down MPF, CCQs, and anticipate problems.
5. **Map lesson stages.** Don't write yet—just sketch the flow.
6. **Draft the plan.** Use my skeleton template.

7. **Script key moments.** Think through instructions, examples, and ICQs.
8. **Practice timing.** Rehearse any clarification or demo stage.

Following this system helped me plan in 90 to 120 minutes instead of 4 hours.

Reflection Tools

I created a reflection table that I completed after each TP. It included:

- What went well
- What didn't go well
- Key student reactions
- Tutor feedback
- Action points for next time

This made writing Assignment 4 much easier and improved the quality of my lesson planning across the course.

Trainee Tip: Your reflection notes are your development history. Take them seriously. They will inform your final assignment and your long-term teaching habits.

File Management

You'll accumulate dozens of files over the course. Here's how I organised mine:

- **Folder: CELTA Course**
    - Subfolder: TPs (TP2 to TP8, each with plan, materials, self-reflection)
    - Subfolder: Assignments (Drafts and Final)
    - Subfolder: Input Notes
    - Subfolder: Tutor Feedback
    - Subfolder: Grammar Resources

Good organisation = lower cognitive load. When you're tired, anxious, or behind, being able to find the right file immediately matters.

Physical Tools (If You're Onsite)

If your CELTA is face-to-face, you may also benefit from:

- A ring binder or accordion folder for paper copies
- Highlighters for marking tutor comments
- Index cards for cueing instructions or vocabulary
- A portable whiteboard marker set (in case your centre is under-resourced)

Templates to Utilize and Adapt

Every CELTA trainee should build their own versions of the following:

- Lesson planning skeleton
- MPF analysis template
- Controlled and freer task template
- Error correction checklist
- Self-reflection form

These not only save time—they help you standardise your thinking and improve consistency.

Checkpoint: If planning still takes more than three hours by TP5, you likely need to streamline your process. Build a workflow. Cut redundant steps. Focus only on what supports your aim.

In the next chapter, I'll explore how I managed my time, emotions, and mental stamina. CELTA is not just about knowledge—it's about keeping your balance as the pace intensifies.

CHAPTER 7: TIME MANAGEMENT AND BURNOUT PREVENTION

You don't pass CELTA just by working hard. You pass it by working strategically. Burnout is real, and it hits faster than most expect. This chapter shares how I managed my time, reduced decision fatigue, and protected my energy across the most demanding parts of the course.

The CELTA Time Trap

The CELTA workload is unrelenting. Most trainees start strong but falter by midway when the demands pile up:

- Teaching Practice preparation
- Assignments with strict deadlines
- Live input sessions
- Ongoing feedback and planning revisions

The mistake I saw repeatedly? Trainees trying to do everything, every day, at maximum intensity. That's not sustainable.

Trainer Insight: "You're being trained as a teacher, not tested as a robot. If you collapse halfway through the course, your knowledge doesn't matter."

How I Structured My Week

By halfway, I developed a fixed weekly rhythm that reduced decision fatigue.

Monday to Friday:

- Morning: Input sessions and notes
- Afternoon: Assignment work or planning (depending on the week)
- Evening: Review lesson feedback, grammar revision, or rehearsal

Saturday (Teaching Practice Day):

- Morning: Final prep and delivery
- Afternoon: Group feedback session
- Evening: Reflection + rest

Sunday:

- 2–3 hours of planning for the upcoming week
- 1 hour for reviewing assignment feedback or tutor comments
- Full evening off to recharge

Time-Saving Habits That Worked

1. **Set timers for planning sessions.** I used 90-minute blocks followed by a 10-minute break. This prevented over-polishing and kept momentum.
2. **Batch tasks.** I grouped similar tasks together. For example:

- Created all CCQs for a lesson in one sitting
- Did MPF analysis across all target phrases before scripting lesson stages
  3. **Pre-scheduled peer check-ins.** I booked Zoom calls with fellow trainees in advance to review plans, which reduced last-minute panic.
  4. **Automated what I could.** I saved boilerplate lesson plan language (e.g., lead-in descriptions, ICQ patterns) in a document for quick adaptation.

Trainee Tip: If you're "improving" a plan three hours before teaching, you're not improving it. You're second-guessing. Submit. Move on.

How I Managed Energy (Not Just Time)

You can have a perfectly structured day—and still burn out. The real battle is emotional. Here's how I protected my mental bandwidth:

- **Planned breaks as seriously as tasks.** I scheduled time to walk, nap, or call family.
- **Had boundaries with peers.** I didn't engage in group chats past 9:00 PM. Constant CELTA talk drains you.
- **Practised mental switching.** I used a short routine (music, a coffee, or a short YouTube clip) to shift gears between tasks.
- **Celebrated wins.** After each TP, I recorded a 30-second voice note to myself about what went well. This helped balance the pressure of ongoing feedback.

Trainer Insight: "Tired teachers talk more, reflect less, and lose clarity. Protect your thinking time above all."

Red Flags That You're Burning Out

Watch for these signs:

- Feeling unable to switch off even after submitting work
- Constant self-doubt or catastrophizing feedback
- Avoiding planning or leaving it until late at night
- Rewriting lesson plans obsessively after they've been approved

If this happens, reset. You need to:

- Speak to your tutor. They would rather support you than see you burn out.
- Take a real break—even a 12-hour window off CELTA can help.
- Focus only on the next deliverable. Ignore anything beyond 48 hours ahead.

Checkpoint: CELTA is not a marathon. It's a series of tightly timed sprints. Run each one, rest, and refocus.

Practical Recovery Strategies

- **Low-input evenings:** Watch a movie in English to keep your ear tuned but your brain relaxed.
- **Set a shutdown routine:** End your workday the same way each night (e.g., shut laptop, write to-do for tomorrow, turn off notifications).
- **One-tab rule:** When planning or writing, keep only one browser tab open. This curbs distraction.
- **Limit social media:** Create a separate profile if needed—disconnect your main one.

What I'd Do Differently

Looking back, I would:

- Take every Sunday evening off without guilt
- Spend less time reformatting plans and more time scripting instructions

- Prioritise health: sleep, hydration, and walking saved me from spiralling

Trainee Tip: Perfectionism is the enemy of progress. CELTA tutors don't want you to be brilliant—they want you to be *developing*.

In the next chapter, we'll look beyond CELTA. I'll share how I transitioned into real teaching roles, how the CELTA gave me a competitive edge, and what came next in my career—from IELTS examiner to university lecturer.

CHAPTER 8: LIFE AFTER CELTA

CELTA ends quickly—but its effects last for years. The intensity, structure, and feedback can make the four-week course feel like a full academic year compressed into a single month. But what happens next? How do you turn this qualification into real teaching work?

In this chapter, I'll share what life looked like for me after CELTA, how the certificate opened doors, and what I learned navigating jobs, interviews, and professional growth.

What CELTA Prepares You For

CELTA equips you with more than just classroom skills. It trains you to:

- Think like a professional teacher
- Analyse learner needs in real time
- Plan lessons around outcomes, not just topics
- Receive and act on feedback

By the end of the course, you'll have:

- Taught between 6–8 observed lessons
- Completed four assessed written assignments

- Received tutor feedback on every aspect of your development

You'll also be more confident, more reflective, and more adaptable than when you began.

Trainer Insight: "CELTA doesn't make you a perfect teacher. It gives you the mindset and tools to *become* one, lesson by lesson."

My Post-CELTA Trajectory

After CELTA, I was offered an IELTS examiner role and later took up a position as an Assistant Professor at a university in South Korea. These roles were not automatic—but CELTA played a pivotal role in making me credible, prepared, and employable.

Here's how the course translated into opportunities:

- My Teaching Practice reflections gave me strong examples to use in interviews.
- The detailed lesson planning experience gave me confidence to talk about syllabus design and learner engagement.
- My improved grammar knowledge (thanks to the Language Related Tasks assignment) meant I could explain language clearly under pressure—something IELTS examiners must do.

Finding Work After CELTA

There are three major employment routes post-CELTA:

1. **Language schools:**
   - General English, exam prep, or business English
   - Often in Europe, Asia, or Latin America
   - Contracts range from 6 months to 2 years
2. **International programs:**
   - IELTS prep, university pathway programs, summer schools

- Typically higher pay and more structured training
3. **Online teaching:**
  - Platforms like iTalki, Preply, or private contracting
  - Flexible hours, growing demand

Websites to check:

- www.tefl.com
- www.tefl.net
- www.jobs.ac.uk (for UK college and university posts)
- www.eslcafe.com
- Jobs sections of British Council and International House

Your First Job: What to Expect

Most CELTA graduates begin with General English classes or beginner/intermediate learners. You may teach from a set textbook (e.g., Cutting Edge, English File, or Headway) with some room for creativity.

Key takeaways:

- You'll probably teach more hours than on CELTA, but with less pressure.
- You won't be observed every day, but internal observations will happen.
- You'll have to adapt your CELTA knowledge to new environments.

Trainee Tip: Your first job is not about proving brilliance. It's about applying the CELTA method consistently while learning your new environment.

Transitioning From CELTA to Real Classrooms

What changes:

- Fewer formal reflections
- More autonomy with lesson design
- More pastoral care duties (checking homework, reporting progress)
- Larger class sizes and mixed-ability groups

What stays the same:

- The importance of lesson aims
- The need to grade your language
- The benefit of reflection after each class
- The value of student-centred interaction

Trainer Insight: The best CELTA graduates aren't the ones who aced every TP. They're the ones who keep refining their practice after the certificate is in hand.

What CELTA Doesn't Teach (But You Can Learn)

1. **Long-term course planning:** In real jobs, you may need to map out a term or syllabus.
2. **Classroom discipline strategies:** Especially with teenagers or larger classes.
3. **Administrative duties:** Attendance logs, grading reports, parent meetings.
4. **Technology integration:** CELTA may touch on this, but jobs often require digital fluency.

How to upskill post-CELTA:

- Attend webinars (e.g., Cambridge English, IATEFL, ELT webinars)
- Take specialist certificates (e.g., Young Learners, Business English)
- Observe experienced teachers in your institution

Professional Development After CELTA

CELTA is just the beginning. Many teachers go on to:

- Take the DELTA (Diploma in Teaching English to Adults)
- Complete MA TESOL or related qualifications
- Move into academic management or teacher training
- Write materials or develop exams (as I did with IELTS prep books)

Checkpoint: If you're two months post-CELTA and haven't taught yet, don't panic. Apply broadly, stay connected to your cohort, and keep building your CV with online courses, tutoring, or volunteering.

In the final chapter, I'll share bonus tools: templates, checklists, and reflection guides that you can use during CELTA and beyond to stay grounded, consistent, and focused on your teaching journey.

CHAPTER 9: BONUS TOOLS AND TEMPLATES

In this final chapter, I want to give you the tools I wish I had from Day 1. These are not generic templates—they're drawn directly from my CELTA experience, including actual resources I created, how I used them, and what made them effective.

This chapter includes:

- Sample planning and reflection templates
- A PowerPoint walkthrough of actual materials I used in TP
- Visual aid design tips
- Self-assessment checklists to keep your growth on track

Sample TP Planning Template

Below is the basic structure I developed and used for every lesson from TP4 onward.

Lesson Skeleton (Editable in Word or Google Docs):

1. Lesson Aim
2. Sub-Aim

3. Stage-by-Stage Breakdown:
    - Stage
    - Procedure
    - Timing
    - Interaction (T-S, S-S, S-S-T)
    - Rationale
4. Anticipated Problems and Solutions
5. Materials & Notes

Why it works: This format forced me to justify each stage and helped tutors see my logic clearly. Over time, I could complete this in under 90 minutes.

Language Analysis Table (MPF Template)

Target Language	Meaning	CCQs	Form	Pronunciation	Problems & Solutions
"used to live"	Past habit	"Do I do it now?"	Subject + used to + base verb	/ˈjuːstə/ with weak form	Students confuse with "be used to"; drill with context

Tip: Complete this section **before** designing tasks. It will shape your lead-in, clarification, and CCQs.

How I Used PowerPoint to Strengthen My TP

As part of my online CELTA course, I used custom-designed slide decks for almost every lesson. These slides were not filler—they were **pedagogical scaffolds**.

Here are four examples that had a direct impact on lesson quality:

1. TP4 Vocabulary: Free Time Activities

- Used icon-based visuals to pre-teach phrases like "go hiking," "do yoga," "watch TV."
- Designed a matching task using clickable elements for

student engagement.
- Learner Benefit: Reduced reliance on L1 and improved lexical retention.

2. TP6 Reading: Moral Dilemmas

- Embedded a pre-reading image with discussion questions to activate schemata.
- Gist task slide included three visual options learners had to choose from.
- Learner Benefit: Helped guide their attention and reduced text anxiety.

3. TP7 Listening: TED Talk – Secrets of Success

- Pre-listening vocabulary slides helped front-load key lexis like "persist," "serve," "focus."
- Slide also included CCQs with visual cues.
- Learner Benefit: Increased listening comprehension by anchoring key words.

4. TP8 Vocabulary: Idioms and Figurative Language

- Matching task between idioms and literal images ("cost an arm and a leg," "hold your horses")
- Created a gap-fill slide followed by a pair-share discussion prompt.
- Learner Benefit: Idioms were remembered because learners could visualise them.

Trainee Tip: Don't overfill your slides. Use 80% visuals, 20% text. And always check the layout on the student-facing platform (Zoom, Teams, or classroom projector).

Visual Aid Design Checklist

Use this list to evaluate whether your slides or boardwork will support learning:

- Does each slide have a clear purpose tied to the lesson aim?
- Are key words or phrases highlighted, bolded, or colour-coded?
- Have I rehearsed transitions and checked for tech issues?
- Does every image support—not distract from—the task?
- Have I anticipated which slides might need clarification or simplification?

Self-Reflection Tracker

Create a one-page weekly log to track progress, feedback, and improvement:

- TP Number:
- Main Aim:
- What went well:
- What I would change:
- Tutor feedback highlights:
- Action plan for next TP:

Keep these short. Over time, the trends will emerge—and you'll know exactly where to focus.

Final Thought

No CELTA lesson is perfect. But with the right tools, systems, and mindset, each one can be a step forward. You do not need to impress anyone with innovation. You need to teach clearly, reflect honestly, and improve methodically.

These templates, trackers, and materials made that possible for me—and now they're yours.

Thank you for joining me on this journey. Whether you're starting your CELTA soon, halfway through, or reflecting after, I hope this book helps you feel guided, prepared, and professionally grounded.

BONUS CHAPTER: TRAINER SECRETS – WHAT CELTA TUTORS REALLY LOOK FOR

Having spoken with multiple CELTA tutors and reflected on my own experience, I've distilled what the best assessors truly value in a candidate. These are the behaviours and mindsets that consistently result in strong reports and Pass B/Pass A outcomes.

1. Responsiveness Over Raw Skill

Tutors don't expect you to be perfect. They expect you to respond to feedback. If they mention an issue in TP3 and it's resolved by TP4, that earns more credit than natural teaching flair that doesn't develop.

Tutor Quote: "Improvement matters more than instinct. The candidate who listens, reflects, and adapts is always easier to pass."

2. Consistent Clarity

From lesson aims to CCQs to instruction, clarity wins. Many trainees try to impress with complexity. Tutors are looking for:

- Clear aims that match procedures
- Clear instructions (tested via ICQs)
- Clear boardwork or visual aids

Checklist:

- Is your aim specific and measurable?
- Would a low-level learner understand your task instructions?
- Does your clarification stick to only what learners *need* to know?

---

3. A Calm, Student-Centred Demeanour

Classroom presence matters. You don't have to be loud or charismatic, but you do need to:

- Make students feel safe trying
- Stay calm when tasks go wrong
- Focus on student language, not your own performance

Signs tutors watch for:

- Do you elicit or explain everything yourself?
- Are students engaged and speaking more than you?
- Do you adapt mid-lesson when confusion arises?

---

4. Real Reflection

Tutors can spot box-ticking reflection instantly. They are looking for:

- Specific examples

- Cause-and-effect thinking
- A clear link between reflection and action in future lessons

Example: "I realised my ICQs were too complex, which caused confusion during the controlled task. Next time I'll use yes/no questions and model before asking."

This shows analysis, accountability, and a growth mindset.

5. Professionalism Without Perfectionism

Being organised, punctual, respectful, and consistent matters. But obsessing over every slide, script, or handout to the point of missing deadlines is a red flag. The best trainees know when to say, "Good enough. Time to move on."

Final Tutor Insight: "CELTA doesn't reward brilliance. It rewards reliability. If I had to hire one of my trainees tomorrow, it would be the one who was always prepared, self-aware, and improving—even slowly."

Use these insights not as pressure, but as perspective. Focus on clarity, adaptability, and reflection—and you will not just pass CELTA. You'll leave it ready for any classroom.

Good luck on your journey!

ENJOYED THIS BOOK? PLEASE LEAVE A 5-STAR REVIEW

If CELTA Made Easy helped you survive the course, deepen your teaching, or approach the classroom with more confidence—I'd be genuinely grateful if you could leave a 5-star review on Amazon.

Your feedback not only helps other future CELTA candidates find the book, but also supports independent publishing from real teachers who have walked the same path.

Even a single sentence can make a big difference.

Thank you for reading—and for being part of this growing, global teaching community.
Daniel James
Author, *CELTA Made Easy* and *IELTS Speaking: Idioms & Phrasal Verbs for Band 7+*

BOOKS BY THIS AUTHOR

Teaching Ielts Speaking: Examiner Insights And Classroom Strategies For Maximizing Student Performance

Teach IELTS Speaking with Clarity, Confidence, and Examiner Insight
Tired of vague teaching guides that don't actually show you how to help your students succeed?
Written by a former IELTS Speaking examiner, this practical, no-nonsense handbook gives teachers exactly what they've been missing: clear, structured, and insight-driven strategies to prepare students for the real test.

Whether you're an experienced instructor or new to IELTS, this guide will transform the way you teach Speaking—one lesson, one learner, and one band score at a time.

Band 7+ Ielts Speaking: Idioms & Phrasal Verbs Made Easy: A 30-Day Plan To Build Natural Vocabulary And Impress The Examiner

This practical, examiner-informed guide is your complete toolkit for mastering idioms and phrasal verbs — two essential ingredients for a high score in IELTS Speaking.

Designed for learners aiming for Band 7 or above, this book includes:

373 carefully selected idioms with clear meanings and examples

260 phrasal verbs used in natural, test-style contexts

A 30-day study plan with daily prompts, vocabulary targets, and speaking practice

Real IELTS-style questions to help you activate new expressions

Reflection tasks to reinforce what you've learned

Examiner tips to help you sound fluent, natural, and in control

Whether you're preparing on your own or looking for extra support between lessons, this book will show you exactly how to use idiomatic language without sounding memorised or unnatural.

Every page is designed to build confidence, fluency, and lexical range — the keys to unlocking your Band 7+.

Ielts Speaking Tips From An Examiner: Insider Secrets And Strategies To Master The Ielts Speaking Test

IELTS Speaking Tips from an Examiner – Insider Secrets to Master the Test
Unlock Your Full Potential in the IELTS Speaking Test!

Are you struggling with the IELTS Speaking test? Confused about what examiners are really looking for? Want to maximize your band score with proven techniques?

Written by a former IELTS examiner, this book reveals the

exact strategies used to assess candidates—giving you insider knowledge to achieve your dream score!

Printed in Dunstable, United Kingdom

63960203R00038